EXPLORING COUNTRIES

Norway

by Derek Zobel

BELLWETHER MEDIA • MINNEAPOLIS, MN

Note to Librarians, Teachers, and Parents:

Blastoff! Readers are carefully developed by literacy experts and combine standards-based content with developmentally appropriate text.

Level 1 provides the most support through repetition of high-frequency words, light text, predictable sentence patterns, and strong visual support.

Level 2 offers early readers a bit more challenge through varied simple sentences, increased text load, and less repetition of high-frequency words.

Level 3 advances early-fluent readers toward fluency through increased text and concept load, less reliance on visuals, longer sentences, and more literary language.

Level 4 builds reading stamina by providing more text per page, increased use of punctuation, greater variation in sentence patterns, and increasingly challenging vocabulary.

Level 5 encourages children to move from "learning to read" to "reading to learn" by providing even more text, varied writing styles, and less familiar topics.

Whichever book is right for your reader, Blastoff! Readers are the perfect books to build confidence and encourage a love of reading that will last a lifetime!

This edition first published in 2012 by Bellwether Media, Inc.

No part of this publication may be reproduced in whole or in part without written permission of the publisher. For information regarding permission, write to Bellwether Media, Inc., Attention: Permissions Department, 5357 Penn Avenue South, Minneapolis, MN 55419.

Library of Congress Cataloging-in-Publication Data
Zobel, Derek, 1983-
Norway / by Derek Zobel.
  p. cm. – (Exploring countries) (Blastoff! readers)
Summary: "Developed by literacy experts for students in grades three through seven, this book introduces young readers to the geography and culture of Norway"–Provided by publisher.
Includes bibliographical references and index.
ISBN 978-1-60014-620-6 (hardcover : alk. paper)
1. Norway–Juvenile literature. I. Title.
DL409.Z63 2012
948.1–dc22   2011002228

Printed in the United States of America, North Mankato, MN.

080111   1187

Contents

Did you know?
Norway means "the northern way." It is named for its location in the northern part of the world.

Norwegian Sea

N
W   E
S

Sweden

Finland

Norway

Oslo ★

Skagerrak Strait

North Sea

Denmark

4

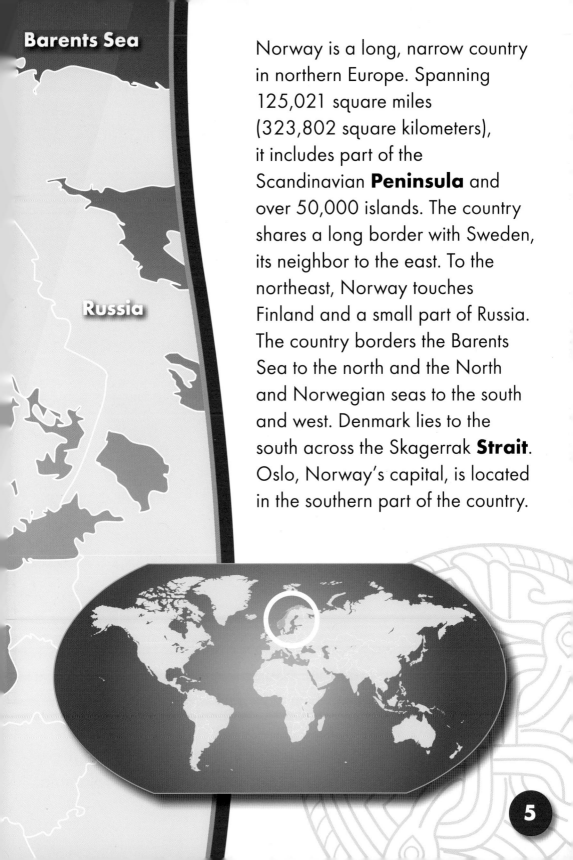

Barents Sea

Russia

Norway is a long, narrow country in northern Europe. Spanning 125,021 square miles (323,802 square kilometers), it includes part of the Scandinavian **Peninsula** and over 50,000 islands. The country shares a long border with Sweden, its neighbor to the east. To the northeast, Norway touches Finland and a small part of Russia. The country borders the Barents Sea to the north and the North and Norwegian seas to the south and west. Denmark lies to the south across the Skagerrak **Strait**. Oslo, Norway's capital, is located in the southern part of the country.

Most of Norway is covered in mountains. The Lang Mountains are the main mountain range of the country. They start in southern Norway and stretch into the north. One of the only flat areas in the country is the Jaeren Plain in the southwest. Beaches line the coast where the plain meets the sea. Norway's major river is the Glomma.

Norway is famous for its **fjords**. These long, narrow inlets of the sea extend for miles into Norway's land. Thousands of years ago, melting **glaciers** carved Norway's landscape, including the fjords. Sogn Fjord, in southwestern Norway, stretches for 128 miles (206 kilometers) and is the longest fjord in the country.

fun fact

If tourists want to visit Svalbard, they have to take a boat. No planes can land on the islands!

Svalbard is an **archipelago** that lies in the Arctic Ocean, between the mainland of Norway and the **North Pole**. The archipelago covers 24,209 square miles (62,700 square kilometers) and includes nine main islands. The largest island is Spitsbergen. Snowy mountains and vast plains cover Svalbard's landscape.

Did you know?
Svalbard means "cold coast." In the winter, temperatures on Svalbard can be -40° Fahrenheit (-40° Celsius).

In the 1600s and 1700s, **whalers** from countries around the world came to Svalbard to hunt for whales. Miners first came to the islands in the late 1800s to dig for coal. Many **expeditions** into the **Arctic**, especially to the North Pole, have been based out of Svalbard.

reindeer

Norway is home to a wide variety of wildlife. Reindeer, elk, lemmings, and martens roam the forests and plains. They must watch out for bears, wolves, lynx, and other predators. Wolverines stalk prey throughout many parts of Norway, but they are most common in the north.

wolverine

lynx

basking shark

! fun fact
Basking sharks open their mouths
and swim forward when they
are hungry. They catch small
animals called plankton.

Many kinds of **aquatic** wildlife live in and around Norway.
Salmon, trout, and other fish swim in the country's rivers.
The seas and fjords around Norway have many ocean
animals, including sperm whales and basking sharks.

Sami people

Did you know?

The Vikings are ancestors of the Norwegian people. They were skilled sailors, warriors, and shipbuilders who explored the seas of northern Europe.

Norway is home to more than 4.5 million people. Almost all Norwegians have **ancestors** who were **native** to the land of Norway. The Sami are a people of Norway who are known for herding reindeer and living off the land. Around 60,000 Sami live in the northern part of the country. Other people have ancestors from other European countries. A small number of people are **immigrants**.

Norwegian is the official language of Norway. Small groups of people speak Swedish and Finnish, the languages of Sweden and Finland. The Sami people have their own language, which is official in some parts of Norway.

Speak Norwegian!

English	Norwegian	How to say it
hello	hallo	hah-loo
good-bye	adjø	ah-dewr
yes	ja	yah
no	nei	nah-eye
please	takk	TAHK
thank you	takk	TAHK
friend	venn	vehn

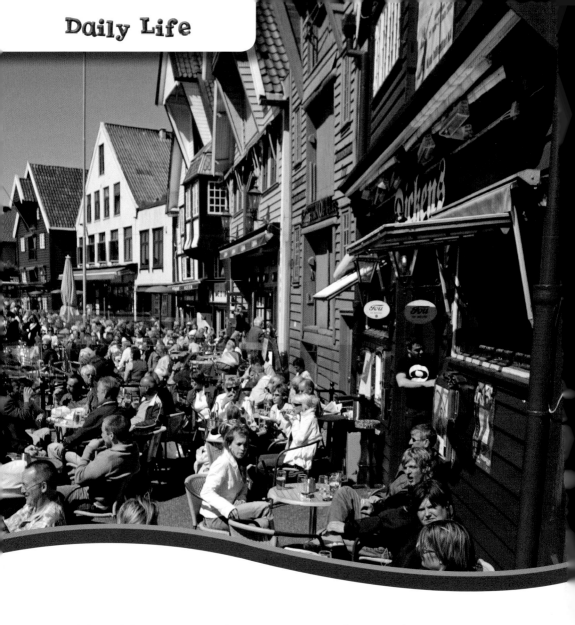

Most Norwegians live in cities in the southern part of the country. Oslo and the surrounding **suburbs** are home to almost 1.5 million people. They live in apartments or houses and shop at supermarkets, open-air markets, and many kinds of stores.
To get around, people use trains, cars, and buses.

In the countryside, people live in small towns. Some people live in fishing villages along the coast. People in the countryside shop at local markets or go to larger cities to buy goods. They mostly use cars to get around, but they often travel long distances by train.

Where People Live in Norway

countryside
21%

cities
79%

Children in Norway must attend school from ages 6 to 16. Elementary school lasts for 7 years. Students learn music, history, science, math, and geography during these years. They also study English and Norwegian.

After elementary school, students move on to lower secondary school and then upper secondary school. Those who graduate can go to a **vocational school** to receive specific job training. They can also attend a university.

Did you know?

Most schools in Norway, including vocational schools and universities, are free for students to attend.

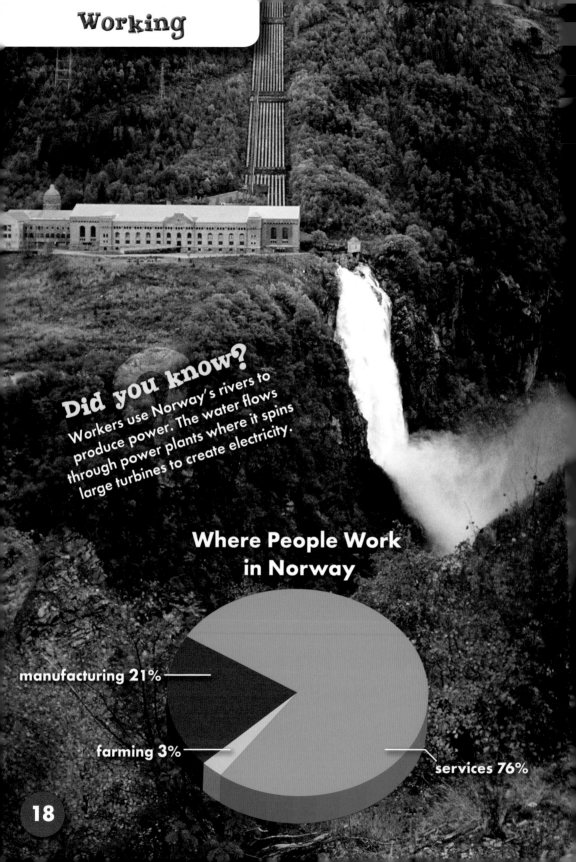

Did you know?

Workers use Norway's rivers to produce power. The water flows through power plants where it spins large turbines to create electricity.

Where People Work in Norway

manufacturing 21%

farming 3%

services 76%

Most Norwegians have **service jobs** in Oslo and other cities. They work in offices, restaurants, schools, and other places. Cities also have many factories where workers make chemicals, paper products, and other goods. These items are shipped all over the world. In coastal cities, many Norwegians find work as fishermen or in **shipyards**.

Many Norwegians work to gather Norway's **natural resources**. Miners dig up **minerals** and send them to the factories in the cities. Workers drill for oil and **refine** it into gasoline and other products. Very few Norwegians are farmers. Those who do farm grow grains and potatoes or raise cattle and pigs. Some raise dairy cows to make milk and cheese.

fun fact

Norway has won more medals at the Winter Olympics than any other country in the world.

The cold weather and year-round snow make skiing the most popular sport in Norway. Many people enjoy cross-country and downhill skiing. Others like to ice skate and play hockey. Norwegian athletes do well in many of these sports at the **Olympics**.

Norwegians also use their free time to read, watch movies, and go to museums. They enjoy listening to music and sharing traditional folktales. Many people own homes in the countryside where they go when they want to relax.

A lot of Norwegian meals feature seafood caught from the surrounding seas. Many dishes include salmon, trout, cod, shrimp, and herring. *Torsk* is a favorite main dish throughout the country. It is **poached** cod that is served with potatoes and melted butter. **Pickled** herring is often enjoyed with bread or crackers. *Fiskesuppe* is a popular soup that can use any kind of fish. It is made with milk, carrots, onions, potatoes, and other vegetables.

Beef, pork, and other meats are also used in many dishes. Meatballs, or *kjøttkaker*, and sausages are regularly served at lunch and dinner. For dessert, people enjoy blueberries, lingonberries, and other fruits. They sometimes eat traditional Christmas cookies, or *krumkake*. These cookies are rolled very thin and filled with whipped cream.

fun fact

Many Norwegians enjoy *lutefisk*, or fish soaked in a chemical called lye. The fish has to be washed clean before it can be cooked and eaten!

kjøttkaker

lefse

Did you know?

Lefse is a Norwegian flatbread made from potatoes, flour, and milk or cream. It is cooked on a griddle and often eaten with butter, sugar, or fish.

23

Constitution Day

Most Norwegians are Christians. They celebrate Christmas, Easter, and other Christian holidays. During the Christmas season, houses and towns are decorated with wreaths, trees, and lights. Families attend church on Christmas Eve. After church, they go home and have a large meal. They often dance around their trees while singing Christmas carols.

Norway also has holidays that mark important events in its history. On May 17, Norwegians celebrate Constitution Day. On this day in 1814, the country's **constitution** was signed into law. In cities across the country, children wave flags and parade down the streets.

In the late fall and early spring, people in Norway can often see the Aurora Borealis, or the northern lights. These bright waves of red, green, and yellow streak through the atmosphere at night. They are best viewed in the Arctic.

Many people travel to the city of Tromsø or the islands of Lofoten to see these lights. Some cities offer tours that take people to the best viewing areas. Many people rent snowmobiles and follow the northern lights across the sky. The northern lights are a symbol of the north and a part of Norway's long history.

Fast Facts About Norway

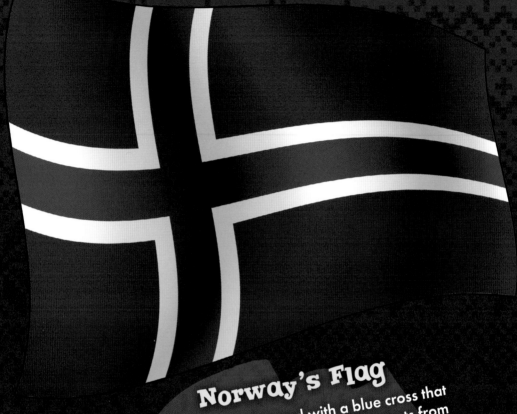

Norway's Flag

The flag of Norway is red with a blue cross that is outlined in white. It is a mix of elements from the flags of Sweden and Denmark. After Norway separated from Sweden, the flag was officially adopted on December 15, 1899.

Official Name: Kingdom of Norway

Area: 125,021 square miles (323,802 square kilometers); Norway is the 67th largest country in the world.

Capital City:	Oslo
Important Cities:	Bergen, Trondheim, Stavanger
Population:	4,676,305 (July 2011)
Official Language:	Norwegian
National Holiday:	Constitution Day (May 17)
Religions:	Christian (90.1%), Other (9.9%)
Major Industries:	fishing, manufacturing, mining, services, shipbuilding
Natural Resources:	oil, timber, iron ore, copper, lead, zinc, nickel, natural gas
Manufactured Products:	food products, ships, metals, paper products, chemicals, wood products, clothing
Farm Products:	barley, wheat, potatoes, pork, beef, milk, fish
Unit of Money:	krone; the krone is divided into 100 øre.

Glossary

ancestors—relatives who lived long ago

aquatic—living in water

archipelago—a group of islands

Arctic—the northernmost part of the world; part of Norway lies in the Arctic.

constitution—the basic principles and laws of a nation

expeditions—trips people take for a specific reason; people often go on expeditions to explore unfamiliar lands.

fjords—long, narrow inlets of the ocean between tall cliffs; the movement of glaciers makes fjords.

glaciers—massive sheets of ice that cover a large area of land

immigrants—people who leave one country to live in another country

minerals—elements found in nature; iron ore, copper, and zinc are examples of minerals.

native—originally from a specific place

natural resources—materials in the earth that are taken out and used to make products or fuel

North Pole—Earth's northernmost point

Olympics—international games held every two years; the Olympics alternate between summer sports and winter sports.

peninsula—a section of land that extends out from a larger piece of land and is almost completely surrounded by water

pickled—preserved with pickle; pickle is a liquid that keeps food from spoiling.

poached—cooked in boiling water or another hot liquid

refine—to remove unwanted parts of a material; Norwegian oil workers refine oil to make gasoline and other products.

service jobs—jobs that perform tasks for people or businesses

shipyards—places where ships are built or repaired

strait—a narrow stretch of water that connects two larger bodies of water

suburbs—communities that lie just outside a city

vocational school—a school that trains students to do specific jobs

whalers—people who hunt whales

To Learn More

AT THE LIBRARY

Britton, Tamara L. *Norway*. Edina, Minn.: ABDO Pub., 2002.

Landau, Elaine. *Norway*. New York, N.Y.: Children's Press, 1999.

Wan, Vanessa. *Welcome to Norway*. Milwaukee, Wisc.: G. Stevens, 2004.

ON THE WEB

Learning more about Norway is as easy as 1, 2, 3.

1. Go to www.factsurfer.com.

2. Enter "Norway" into the search box.

3. Click the "Surf" button and you will see a list of related Web sites.

With factsurfer.com, finding more information is just a click away.

Index

The images in this book are reproduced through the courtesy of: Tupungato, front cover; Maisei Raman, front cover (flag), p. 28; Juan Martinez, pp. 4-5, 5 (small), 11 (top), 23 (small), 29; Danita Delimont/Getty Images, p. 6; GagarinART, p. 7; Gail Johnson, p. 8 (small); Witold Kaszkin, pp. 8-9; Minden Pictures/Masterfile, pp. 10-11; Jamen Percy, p. 11 (middle); Wildlife Bildagentur GmbH/KimballStock, p. 11 (bottom); Scanpix Creative/Masterfile, p. 12; Sindre Ellingsen/Alamy, p. 14; Bartosz Koszowski, p. 15; AFP/Getty Images, pp. 16-17; Paul Lawrence/Photolibrary, p. 18; Andrey Tirakhov, p. 19 (left); Yvette Cardozo/Photolibrary, p. 19 (right); Monkey Business Images, p. 20; RABOUAN Jean-Baptiste/Photolibrary, p. 21; Gary John Norman/Getty Images, p. 22; Gus Filgate/Photolibrary, p. 23 (left); Robyn Mackenzie, p. 23 (right); Robert Harding Picture Library Ltd/Alamy, pp. 24-25; Artic Photo/Alamy, pp. 26-27.